The Farmer's Daughter

The Farmer's Daughter

poems by

LYNNELL EDWARDS

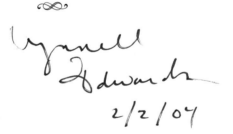

RED HEN PRESS LOS ANGELES

THE FARMER'S DAUGHTER

Some of the poems in this collection first appeared in the following publica-
tions (some were titled slightly differently): "Meanwhile, Back at the Ranch"
in Hubbub; "Coach Sean Faces His Son At Bat" in The Oregonian; "Florida
Prophecy" and "The Professor Prepares His Lecture," and "Noah Afloat" in
Oregon Review; "At Sea" and "Schumann in the Wings" (both forthcoming fall
2003) in Poetry East; "Into the Kill Pen in Poetry Motel; "When He Drops Off the
German Teacher at School the Next Morning" in Portland; "Spilt Milk"
(forthcoming) and "June 1" in Rattapallax; "On Telling Myself It Was Not a
Ship of War" in Riven; "Lecture Notes" in Slant.

Cover art "Mother May I?" © 2003 by C. David Jones
Book and cover design: Mark E. Cull

ISBN 1-888996-74-9
Library of Congress Catalog Card Number: 2003094611
Manufactured in Canada

Publication of this volume is made possible in part
through support by the California Arts Council.

Red Hen Press
www.redhen.org

First Edition

for Wes

Table of Contents

I

Juliana To Her Lover   13
Meanwhile, Back at the Ranch   14
Low Tide   15
At Sea   16
The Sailor Considers the Sand   17
Adrift   18
When He Drops Off the German Teacher
    at School the Next Morning   19
Long Weekend   20
Before the Light Turns Green   21
Schumann in the Wings   22
Sexing the Poet   23
Barista Boy Blues   24
Sleeping with Rilke;
    or, The German Lover   25
Packing, As If For a Funeral   26

II

The Farmer's Daughter;
    or, Persephone's Return   29
Into the Kill Pen   30
Beasts of Burden   31
Where the Barnyard Ends   32
Parable of the Tenants   33
Fixing Fence on Christmas Day   34
Farm Wife   35
Tenant Boy   36
Spilt Milk   37
Land Management   38
Interruption   39
Song of the Easy Life   40

III

Florida Prophecy   43
This Time Delilah   44
On Telling Myself It Was Not a Ship of War   45
My Sylvia Plath Poem   46
Bianca, The Queen of Mean   47
Noah Afloat   48
Coach Sean Faces His Son at Bat   49
The Professor Prepares His Lecture   50
The Matter at Hand;
    or, We Shall All Hang Separately   51
Workshop Poem; or, Sorry, Austin   52
December 19   53
Song of Hannah's Daughters   54
Hands   56
Lasik Surgery; or, Under the Knife   57
Lecture Notes   58
Success and What You Make of It   59
Andrea with Scarf   60
I Love You   61
June 1   62
Summer Chorus   63

The Farmer's Daughter

I

Juliana To Her Lover

From my still morning porch I see
across the green mown field

to the shade where you walk
to the truckbed and back

to the far door. What have you forgotten?
Your busy form stills to look

toward the barn. Then you reach
again for a chain, a rope,

some wire that might hold
the shadow to the man

when the noon sun rages
and I call across the hay:

I am ready now, come. I am
waiting now, here.

Meanwhile, Back at the Ranch

She wants his drink now, coveting
the icy clink of it sweating
in the thick summer grass. She wants
to taste some of what he has,
lemon or bitter or sweet. She doesn't
even know if it is amber or clear or dark,
but she will reach her warm arm across
his towel now, while the big, bright sun
moves closer to the big, white mountain.
She imagines his laughing protest:
this is mine   get your own   as if to prove
everything she can see really is hers,
everything from the tip of the winking peak
to the very center of his aching skin.

Low Tide

The sea edging out from the shore
imagines the moon would rise and relent

the earthy tug at her frayed hem. Grasping
at crab knuckles and shells, milky glass bits,

tufted, rusting foam she crests with
an empty gasp, bowing again and again

into the cuff of transparent silt,
slipping, rough, into the edge of entropy.

At Sea

So now this one has pulled you up the coast,
wooed you like the tide with her moonsong
into the cold Chesapeake Bay. A four-day sail
from warm Miami, you rattled on the waves
just ahead of the hurricanes. The wind was good.
How far flung they find you: Annapolis, Ireland,
Sidney, even the thick middle of green Tennessee.
You are the satellite; they are the stars. You are
the cloud and they the sky on which you hang.
You are the whirling chaff, they the intemperate wind.
Now you are moored under steely skies, the lines
tight, the rigging secure, and to stay afloat you paint
tin roofs while the rain slashes your back, your hands.
You tend bar late and think of ways to tell your friends
you won't be returning; you enumerate the ways to tie a knot.
But you are dreaming of Miami, the blue the white
the shouts across the morning harbor light and free.
The splash of language (*hola compadre!*) on the docks;
the flash of sea life schooling at your bow and the dazzle
of heat warping the horizon. And you lift your head
in the Maryland gray to hear them calling again and again:
My man with the little boy's name, come home;
my sea-sick second son, come home. To these arms,
this hearth, come home, my love, to these rocks.

The Sailor Considers the Sand

But still the next day is bright
even after last night
when he thanked her in the dark
for her touch.

O such a beggar she makes of him.

Humbled under her hands,
her mouth, smooth
sail of her back, warm
bow of her thigh
he might cry
out apology

when she slides
into the tide
of dreams that rock
her again
away and back and away
from him

castaway, blinking
on the glittering shore.

Adrift

At seven, the garage door rises
and she catches him with her beams

where he stands shirtless
at the icebox, hunched and grasping.

He offers a small wave, his hand
a worried buoy clanging a last defense

against the roar and verging brightness.
And then the quiet crests between them where

they float adrift on the reckless
current, awash in the frantic tide.

When He Drops Off the German Teacher
at School the Next Morning

Maybe he manages *liebe Imke* when
he pulls the fringed end of her scarf

toward him in the idling car. Maybe
he says *I'm sorry* when she gathers her books

and leans to the door, uncertain how to work the lock.
Maybe he touches her cheek before

he finally just takes his kiss. *Kiss bitte,*
he says. And her cold cheeks burn

when she steps to the yellow curb
where the children have gathered to watch.

Long Weekend

Driving around in her car alone, too early
to pick up the kid at the party, too late
to go anywhere, to buy anything, she finds
an exit, a way down one road south where
she can travel a few miles and then return
the same way north. From her on-ramp vantage
the little signs wink and flash, the knot of road
unravels, and she thinks of that painting
from art class, the one of a woman
crouched in the grass, looking toward
a great, distant house. And she remembers
there is a whole other day in this weekend,
a whole other world's turn of driving
toward horizons, anywhere but home.

Before the Light Turns Green

It's raining Brady, she has written in a hand
that swims on the page of the letter beside him,

and the air has now turned cold. He thinks
about how far away that wet coast is

where she marks the days without him.
He thinks how the noon glare makes

him squint, and how the car ahead won't
move. And he decides to send her flowers,

blooming suns, soft petals, like her hair
he says aloud and smiling now he grasps

the wheel, turns hard. The letter slides,
the motor coughs, the light has changed.

Schumann in the Wings

He must have been transcendent
with desire to write the thousand notes,
each *fantasie* more breathless than the last
for her, his precious, blooming Clara,
genius at the keys, a virtuouso flushed,
upright, grand beyond her faint nine years.
Tonight she lives his passion as
it swarms across staffs black with music
that throbs like bees, hovering, imminent.
Her white hands ache across the octaves,
over and over to the pulse of *des Abends.*
He waits, *furiouso,* for the verging end;
he will have her again, blushless, spent.

Sexing the Poet

I'm with the poet now. I'm with him now
at lunch and he is talking about form,
the freedom of the form, the splendid strain,
the sureness of the ten beat line. He talks
to me about the poem's felt demand, what asks
to be released, the swagger and the show
of what ambition brings at twenty-two.

And as I write and watch and drink my tea,
wild (*ohh*) sweet (*ahhh*) orange, so hot I only
take the smallest taste between my nods,
my careful (*yes*), tracing hands will
work the shadow of his voice I want
to catch and hold, this poet I am
sitting here with now, (*now*) watching.

Barista Boy Blues

Next please next and barista boy coaxes out an es-press-oh
for the ladies and their babies as they shake and they stamp
when they come in from the rain and the gray and the everyday
we go this way to just get by the morning, to just get
one more hit, one more look at the grinding and the flexing,
the slow release of strong arms pulling down and pressing out
and they can hardly stand it, how much longer how much longer
when he asks them: do you want biscotti and do you want it wet?

Then it's oh-oh-no another dumb mistake and the look from
Cleopatra with the snakey silver rings and the thorny rose tattoo
says no-no-no you get nothing, tonight nothing in the back room,
nothing on the bar, and she will walk out in the rain again,
bare skinned and without him. Without even looking
at his tight heart steaming, without even hearing
his dim voice screaming to pull off the adders and the asps
and to hold back the Nile just rising in his chest.

Sleeping with Rilke; or, The German Lover

The dream of you
traum
in the doorway,
shadow where
I come and go,
that language imminent
in your mouth sounding,
toppling through the room
raum raum
I hear you: *Ich bin*
hier but can not
speak and meaning
recedes, eyes
augen augen augen

wide open

Packing, *As* If For a Funeral

Something to wear each different day
though the days may all be the same:
quiet shoes, soft shirts, one lipstick tucked

into the smallest bag. Something
to read, to write, to mail home.
A rain jacket, a wrap, maybe pictures

if there will be seeing or saying
at the last. And something black,
formal as a made bed, solemn

as glass bottles lined on a tray.
Always something black, patient
and flat in the bottom of the case.

II

The Farmer's Daughter; or, Persephone's Return

On first return, she is *hey boys* and *whatcha doin*
and buckets of fresh milk sent from the big house
where her father leans in the doorway, watching under
the porch light as her swinging form disappears
into the stable of darkness. The low murmer
of beasts tells him she has arrived where the Hardt boys
wait for what they've been promised. Dumb as cattle,
they stand to greet her, tip their caps, and smile
in wide appreciation for the gift,
the farmer's hospitality they will receive.
At this late hour they will have it all, including
you, miss. You sure have grown up pretty.
And in between the fumblings of *let*
me help you with that and *when you were little*
and *just like your momma* the great barn door slides shut
and bales of hay are rearranged and this
is not the rapture she has dreamed, the day
when the fine-boned boy sings his words and they
escape to the city.
                                   But there is laughter sure,
the cackle of a joke turned bad. She hears
the lifting wings of owls above their lofts,
the tied mare stamping in her stall. The bucket
spills but does not fill desire's dull thirst
rising in their throats. And she thinks
of calling to her father scratching out
accounts, waiting at the kitchen table,
water in a silver cup at his right hand.
But she remembers orchards that must be
burdened with their fruit, brown tobacco
hanging down in hands, rows of corn
rattling in the fields. She will endure
these sacrificial months of warmth and green,
the bargain hard, unfairly struck.

Into the Kill Pen

And some steers, he tells me, are dark cutters.
Their meat is stained dark, almost black,
by a toxin released to the blood before slaughter.

You can tell, before; they are the nervous type.
Too quick in the stall, the way they jolt
and stamp, stare wild and aware around the ring

or when they move into the chute.
They buck and pace when you load them
frantic into the kill pen, bellowing.

This, he continues, you want to breed out.
This meat is useless, tough and bitter,
a year's feed gone to waste.

Our animals here are all docile, slow.
Their thick heads and shaggy flanks are still.
You could kick them like dogs.

Beasts of Burden

First, the horses, shaggy and silent steaming
in the winter yard or idling in the sun.
Also the cats, under the steps, or into the tool shed,
all hiss and claw and shining eyes.
And the lesser beasts: mice, surprised by light;
starlings assembled in the yard; hogs, bunched
around the trough. And always the cattle.
Bellowing in the night fields outside my window,
standing at odd angles in the barns and pens
as if stopped mid-beat in some ancient reel,
as if there were purpose to their posture,
as if I could hear their brute intelligence as it
echoes across the rafters, lofts over the granaries,
calls out to their mute and impotent god.

Where the Barnyard Ends

On three sides now tract houses push against
the forage field like a line of crooked teeth,

each one fronted with a concrete porch, each
one propped by hollow column, a gabled façade.

The short back yards are littered with broken-
wheeled bikes, blue plastic pools, chipped clay planters.

Dirty balls wedge under new wire fences that keep
the cattle out, but do not stop the dumb beasts

from peering through the night windows, shadeless
and smudged, where the occupants stammer and stare

across indistinct meals, the colorless feed
of their weak-chinned sons, their barren girls.

Parable of the Tenants

The young tenants always drink,
and their dented pick-ups are always
littered with wrappers and cans, rags
stained dark from their last abuse.
They spend nights plotting
on the cracked porch of their little house,
the one at the end of the road,
back furthest on the property,
the one by the barn.
And they show up for work, *goddamn* it.
Mornings they wait in the big circle drive
leaning against their idling trucks,
crossed arms knotty and tight
as a coil of wire, thin hair matted
under broken-billed caps. They kick
the gravel, stamping out the butt ends
of spent cigarettes. They wait
for the litany of orders, *alright*,
the commands to plow and repair,
to sweat below the raging noon sun
when it strafes the rows of hay.
And they look for the landowner's son,
that son of a bitch, to emerge,
smooth-skinned, direct
with his water-clear words,
and they tear him from limb
to outstretched limb.

Fixing Fence on Christmas Day

When the call comes before dawn
that cattle are out again, he throws
the heavy shears and a bale of wire
into the bed of the truck, ignites the engine,
and with a cup of black coffee balanced on the dash
rumbles toward the breach. As he drives
he thinks that there are harder things to do,
chores more tedious, more abusive.
Done right, he knows it is a quick job,
even satisfying to stretch the line of wire,
twist the ends behind the post,
clip and bend them down.

But still, kneeling there this morning
in the cold field he second guesses his work:
what gap will he leave? And not how, but when
will *those damn cows* find the one weak strand
and work the wire into a wide place, force
their thick hides, their soft stomachs through,
and then trot away, stunned stupid
at the unfenced expanse under their hooves?

Now they have massed around him as he works.
They stand lock-kneed and steaming
in the dark and do not spook or scatter.
He meets their eyes with the intelligence of tools,
the prescience of salvation, and resumes repair
on his part of the bargain.

Silent, ungentle beasts who never did speak,
and have never had to answer to him, or the fence,
or the illuminated night slipping from the sky.

Farm Wife

Maybe the best thing about the farm
was dairy delivery. Never to carry

those awkward boxes, never
to make a late run to the store, because

every Tuesday and Saturday morning
there on the back steps, the fare:

two gallons of two percent, one cottage cheese,
one sour cream, a blank receipt.

But really it breaks her heart to see
the dawn each day. The mad orange tear

widening above the barn sighs just like defeat
when all it brings is the same gray news,

flattened and damp, and those cold cartons
waiting, patient as cattle standing.

Tenant Boy

This was the right: to hand down
thin shirts, dark shoes,
scuffed toy trucks and books defaced
with *my name* to the mumbling boy,
his eyes wide and aware, who
may not drink from the same
fat jar of cold water we keep filled
in our clean, new kitchen.

Spilt Milk

Already done now child, and too quick
spreading across the table face,

a glue-white tide rolling toward
the edges of napkins and plates.

This is the sorrow for reaching
your small arm across for more,

and now everyone watching you.
Everyone sees what you have done,

this flat tragedy still
as the tearless end of day,

pooling and cold on the kitchen floor.

Land Management

We own all this land now, he tells me.
From that far, stone fence clear
to the falling barn you see in the East,

we have access now from the road,
frontage of our own, to the back fields
and on to where we join up to the Hardt place.

It looks like nothing, he says,
this slim strip of land, barren as
an old woman, hard with frost

and the brown smack of winter. We would
never plant this piece or think of grazing.
But now trespassers cannot encroach

on our property where they might burn
fires, scare the cattle, or just walk,
wander here without right or title.

Interruption

After a long winter away, I arrive
in my friend's summer kitchen, where

a steaming artichoke bobs
in her black, soup kettle.

She is teaching me to eat
the impossible: one stiff petal at a time,

swirled in yellow translucence,
the faint fragrance of it scraped

with the tip of our teeth. We peel
each leaf in turn, until the damage is

a delicate heap on the counter.
In the doorway her small daughter emerges,

indignant and demanding
the rich choke. She claims

the whole face of it, splashing butter
from the dish and biting though the solid,

center meat, her dark eyes wide,
daring us to take back our prize.

Song of the Easy Life

Your life could be as easy as music.
Light and sweet as cold wine
that pours out singing from a straw carafe;

white-washed blue
like the distant sky
that cradles the afternoon moon;

plenty and sure
as the green-gold harvest
of vines and toppled stalks.

Turn from the fields,
burnt and crumbling
and see heaven's geometry.

Step through the tangle
of wire and wood
that divides this life from another.

See that your days are blessed;
even your shadow winks
with shimmering luck.

Feel how the world wakes
to mornings of light,
and dream that day

when the curtains were raised
on recovery's dark room
and you believed it was time to walk.

III

Florida Prophecy

Were I one for signs on the second day,
I would wait for a perfect sea star
to float across my scuffling feet, and watch

for high arcing porpoises beyond the murmuring
swells. I would consider the lifting gulls,
their assenting formation a visible *yes*,

or the portent crane, one eye on me
staring *no*. But as it is I have
just these few chipped shells knocking

in my loose fist, clinking their little song
of ambivalence, and sounding for all
the world like money in the bank.

This Time Delilah

This time Delilah dream no churning remorse,
no gold-eyed pride when you arc and gasp

into his dark arms. There will be no masking
drapes, no dim halls hung with Philistine ropes.

Tonight he will rest in your lap, smooth-skinned,
thick-curled, all sweet breath, trust, and fatigue.

When he rises, offer your own nape. This time
Delilah let the sword cut clean and bright

across your black tangle falling full, freeing you
of memory and name. Light-headed, stare

straight beyond the stars and lead him
through the open window, careless into Paradise.

On Telling Myself It Was Not a Ship of War

And besides, I liked the way they looked, circled
on the frigate's back deck, six of them in dress whites
brilliant in the sun, caps and creases sharp, black shoes shining.
How could life not be good that day for a guest of the USN?
I watched the river banks slide by, the bow push
the channel into soft furrows, a tumbling wake.
I felt the sun's rich embrace, hot on my back and my face,
and the low roll of progress rumbling at my feet.
This is not without its faults, I thought, notably close berths,
latitudes of silence and horizon, the tedium of duty,
the heaviness of ropes. But it is hard to argue
with a day of filled sails, and confidence cocked back
in a folding chair, hands clasped behind a well-formed head,
the slightest smile, eyes narrowed in the crosshairs.

My Sylvia Plath Poem

She writes poems pre-dawn,
sitting at the window, watching
the moon sink over bleak gardens
and gray steeples. Hag-fingered
trees claw at the horizon
and bones settle in the cold dirt.

How hungry she is
stretching toward full light.
How her thin gut aches
chained to her ashy muse
with the red hair and the red mouth
who swallows whole stanzas
of the best stuff and vomits
it back in approval.

Reports say she burns.
In the morning chill each poem
exacts it jagged pound. Rumors
fly while she shapes each utterance
like a star winking at the white edge
of perfection. Each line
is an apocalypse. Each stanza
a resurrection taking wing.

Now Ted in his bed,
snuffling and warm turns over.
The chatter of children spills
across the cold kitchen floor,
and the day begins, wheezing
and frayed. She is scorched, unrepentant,
falling from an ancient, wheeling sun.

Bianca, the Queen of Mean

She is sprung fury, all screech and fingernails
tearing at the jacket that won't zip, the rain boots
that won't pull. She is Bianca, the Queen of Mean,
who stamps out her place at the coat rack, assumes
the front of the line, all elbows and indignation, and
commands the twisting swings at recess. She will
snatch the sweet grapes from lunchboxes left alone.
She will protest rightful possession of both
the red crayons, all the pink paper. She will
rend her remarkable Valentines:
Bee mine   *Me 4 you*   *U R nice*
hard deliverance to the astounded first grade,
to watching Nolan with the quiet heart, holding
his breath, unfolding the beating card.

Noah Afloat

Alone is the middle of the ocean
where a wilderness of sky and wave

crests in slick walls, bare
and toppling, evolving. Here the wasted

slate of heaven is not punctuated
even by the dove, or the raven

carving wings and curves in relentless dives,
carrying the green sign of communion,

of swelling ground. Just that damn boat,
and the mute beasts of repopulation,

and the wine running out, and the squabbling
sons crowding the bow and berth,

and the water already a stink all around
the splintering hull that rocks unsteady,

a creaking island, ready to explode,
lost in the wake of its own crashing deluge.

Coach Sean Faces His Son at Bat

Coach Sean knuckles the ball, stitched and round
in one cold fist, his coat shut tight, collared high
against the naked April wind. He studies
his son steady at home, white hands tight
on the aluminum bat. And Coach Sean sees
his watching daughter, dark and heavy,
insistence pressed against the sagging fence.
He feels the boys all waiting for the cold clang
that will send the ball relentless over their heads.
They stamp and dance, clattering in their stiff uniforms,
serious under their creased cap bills. They work
their new gloves with pounding fists. And when
the sun breaks strange in the six o'clock sky,
when cars rush through the arc of expectation,
Coach Sean releases, absolves
and whispers to his distant son: run.

The Professor Prepares His Lecture

They fall on their faith so easily, he wonders,
and as he closes the big book of Biology,
he feels the great plates of earth
rolling beneath the gray ocean,
hears the techtonic roar of continents
heaving up mountains in their wake.
He sees the apes falling from trees, scattering
mammals to their underground homes.
He imagines the dumb emergence of uprightness,
the club-gaited march toward wild fire, raging water,
and smiles, there from the apex of Eden.

The Matter at Hand; or,
We Shall All Hang Separately

Friends, colleagues, countrymen, now is the time
when I have called you all together to consider
the matter at hand. If for too long we have stood by
and watched while the train wreck rumbled on, the message
now couldn't be any clearer: we must step up to this pot
that we have stirred. Calling it black will not do.
The red snakes have been raised and the venom-fanged
flags have come back to bite us. Something rotten
this way comes and we are called to be men of action,
women of quick resolve. We must boldly go toward
this matter which has no name, which has no face,
which bobs and weaves in the shadows and waits
for our stammering, punch-drunk reply.
There is no good fight, no full circle, no justice,
in poetry or otherwise, and we must have exactly
the right words then the hammer comes down,
relentless and ringing on our nodding, infant heads.

Workshop Poem; or, Sorry, Austin

One participant said saxophones
are always being asked to do
too much work in poems.

They are always there growling about
sex, and cigarettes smoking alone, it seems
to me. And so, she objected. Another woman

felt that way about cicadas. You know,
she said, they're always there in the background
with their dizzy wings, the infernal saw

of Georgia nights, or Mississippi,
or some godawful Southern swamp. They never work.
Sorry. For me, offered the last, it's bougainvilleas.

And they all agreed. The heavy-scented,
head-filling veil of their pungency, wafting
or whatever, across the veranda, it's predictable.

And then there's that thing about Vietnam,
the association with the Mekong Delta, or bombs,
or I don't know, but bougainvilleas are just

too much. And so there we were,
with the cicadas and the saxophones and the bougainvilleas
roaring around the table, the poem

flat and quiet between us. Our work
here is done, one announced. Thank you
for the generosity of your words.

You, who are tumbling over the couch, arms and legs
flailing into the bookcase, knocking over picture frames,
lamps, the brass globe, glass vases, ceramic bowls.
You, ungrateful sons, already at seven this morning screaming
I hate you curses at one another like dwarfish, battling wizards,
hot lightening flying from the tips of your short fingers, clawing
at one another all the way down the staircase and slamming
into breakfast, barking demands. You, ungrateful boys,
hiding each others' books and games, homework, candy,
lunchboxes, trading insults and accusations like the worst
sort of carnival hack, hell-bent on cheating
the wide-eyed tourist out of his last dime for some cheap trinket
that you cast off as refuse. My love, boys, how long
do you think it will last? Even if it is always Christmas in my heart,
and the lights sparkle over all the snowy places? My love,
boys, how fast it holds against that verging winter equinox,
that starless end of boyhood where you stand
watching, defiant and armed for the cold new year.

Song of Hannah's Daughters

If the promise of a son meant
the promise of that son
would you do it?

Hannah, what did you believe?

Not the last of women (nor the first) to whom
that child comes late, and hard, to arms already
loose and spotted. Not like hapless Eve
and her strident sons who come so fast on temptation
they squabble and knock each other off, not noticing
how the garden walls are already fallen.

Not that pain.

You would bear him and raise him to be
that promise, watch him run faster than the others,
Already at five, he mouths the low vowels of Torah
as he counts clay marbles or draws
wide circles in the dusty yard. You feel
the rumble of the temple in your gut,
watch the solid shadow rise at his back
and sing even more strongly each encroaching
Sabbath of your salvation and your strong god,
His thunder, His judgment.

And still five more would come, each one a candle guttering.

You take him when that day comes, present
him in his boyhood ephod, say his name, *Samuel,*
a whispered, promised prayer that waits alone
near the old man, hearing voices he knows
cannot be yours. He shivers near the altar,
stunned at how he can see from behind
his dark eyes to behind the dark curtain
drawn on the prophet, deaf and blind.

You have saved them all. You have walked
alone to tell how he was brave, how he proclaimed
his readiness, how the elders at Shiloh were amazed
that a boy so slight, the linen loose at his thin waist,
the dark curls still long across his brow, shouldered
the work of the Lord with even breaths, singular vowels.

But the murmur and the clatter of a busy household
that waits to praise you and feast you with hosannahs,
a bounty of wine and oil poured out from jars cracked
open for this day, that raises your name with the jangle of bells,
the clash of cymbals, and the love of the five remaining (but
nothing more is said on this point), signifies nothing today.

Hannah, who did you believe?

We are waiting here for your answer. Tell them
we are here too, one hand like a fist, the other
smooth and light on the backs of our sleeping, infant sons.

Hands

My hands are old before me. Nails thick, opaque.
The skin dark and thin, bunched up in pockets
and lines, deep crosshatching between the thumb
and fore, veins apparent blue, pathological ridges
across the flat back. Scars, a hundred knocks against
a hot stove, a thousand petty lacerations of paper,
and knife, needle and wire. This betrayal of age
makes no claim on able or willing but slyly
waves before my face in prayer or in rage.

Lasik Surgery; or, Under the Knife

It's not just that I won't be able
to see, or that I'll be asked repeatedly
to look at the light, look at the light while
my lids and lashes are in a vice
and a laser rockets toward my eye
to slice my cornea into a geometry
that allows perfect (or near perfect, the surgeon
says, there are no guarantees) vision.
It's that you have called, and have gotten
into my dreams, that other side of sight,
and you are offering free passes, and all
the best, and my mother is calling you
old friend (though mostly mine, she knows)
and I cannot stop time from surging
like the winter river, and I cannot stop
distractions troubling my heart like wind
in the trees. So I will be taking a little pill
for pre-op anxiety (they work, my pharmacist
assures me, he's tried them), and I know
before it's all over there will be pain,
and thick sleep, and phones ringing
in the night. But by tomorrow if anyone
can see better it will be me. I can see
the conspiracy: the surgeon, my mother
the pharmacist, and you. I know how
promises work; I know how
messages are sent. What did you hope to see?

Lecture Notes

I am wearing my best black beret,
round glasses, and driving fast through the rain.
The assault of trucks broad as mammoths
roars past me on the bridge and I prepare
to be contrary to what the Lecturer
has to say. I am certain I know
damn well better what counts; I am
gleefully annoyed at the chance to play
rebel wit, all those other sops
just there to be seen. So settling into
my chair, scratching a few pre-lecture
notes, I see through her obvious point,
her tedious line. Introductions commence,
the throat-clearing cough and *Can you hear me in the back?*
I am near shouting, the heckler's last defense:
We've heard this before. What are the facts?
But it is stammering and din; it is the smallest
storm, my retiring pose to be less alone
in this dim night, raging with the ancient unknown.

Success, and What You Make of It

Traveling along the Sunset Highway at the speed
of, well, sunset, the view is all glare and sparkling
windshield grime. And no matter what deep tunnels
I excavate, the shining end still assaults
my passage, still baffles each impending arrival
at the top of some slick ramp. It is always the end
of the day these days. I think about metaphors for time,
mostly trains come to mind, or railroad, as a verb.
And some will say that it's really the journey
that matters. But for those of us who believe
that destination is all, who like the sun on our backs,
who cannot bear to squint, this road winds and this sun
pulses and these tires whine like the pumping
gasp of some mechanical, aging heart.

Andrea with Scarf

Sitting in the sun at the American soccer park,
Andrea leans back on her hands and takes in
the scene. *Here I am,* she wonders, *doing O.K.*
She is trying to think in English and considers
that word O.K. and does not know what it means.
She watches the children scramble down the field
like a pack of small dogs, or angry munchkins.
That sounds like a German word, and she remembers
the strange movie she saw as a girl in her English class.
A classic Americanisch cinema, her instructor had said,
Over the Rainbow. Well here I am, she smiles,
like in a tornado whirled to this place and sat down
among the American munchkins. She laughs
turning the heads of all the *soccer moms.*
I must tell Katja that word. And she wonders about
her friend who has recently moved to Freiburg.
Liebe Andrea, she wrote in her last letter,
So international here. The children are learning French.
And we try to keep up our English, so
I always write to you in English.

Andrea hears the whistle and watches
the children as they tumble from the field.
The wind picks up and she takes the scarf
belting her waist and knots it loosely
around her neck, *European fashion.*
She pulls down her cap, and squints
at the soccer moms and the American munchkins
and the enormous, cloudless sky where
there are no tornadoes and no rainbow arcing
and she stands to speak with her cheering friends,
I must keep up my American.

I Love You

I hate olives, but buy them for you
from fat jars at that fancy store
where you wish I wouldn't go. I stop up

your mouth with green Peloponnese,
black Kalamatas, purple Mt. Pelions, ripe
baubles with almond or garlic centers,

spicy, cured, or puckered as raisins.
You may taste the far Aegean, salty and blue,
but ladling their liquid brew I can

barely stand the earthy funk. *Olive juice,*
I mouth, wondering and amused
that a deaf lover might be confused,

certain he was seeing something else,
the red-lipped taunt of adoration,
the slick surface of other words.

June 1

No anarchist's screech, no revolution
of spring, indignant and scrambling
into the thin, bleeding dawn. No raw

huzzahs for release from shaggy skins,
rough gloves, the thick winter arms that bind
man to man to machine. It is over.

So far from the frosty nubs of hyacinths, the edge
of green upending the ice, we wonder
about all the angry fuss. We stand tall and exquisite

in watercolor sheathes and loose jackets,
awash in the red bounty of summer, drinking
in the sprawl of it on the broad, afternoon lawn.

Summer Chorus

She skips and slides
in her summer skirt *swish*
like the wish of the breeze on her back.
And her cool white slip
of a shirt says *ahh*
in the endless evening air.
And the candles flicker *ohh*
in the almost breathless twilight.
And the green lawn sparkles *yes*
to the laughter and the splash
and the clink of icy drinks
evanescent sliding down
slender throats and drowning
the bone grinding groan
of bellowing winter gone.

Biographical Note

Lynnell Edwards, Ph.D, is an Associate Professor of English and the Director of the Writing Center and Writing Across the Curriculum programs at Concordia University. Edwards is also a faculty editor for Concordia's literary magazine, *The Promethean*. Her poems have been published in literary journals and anthologies such as *Hubbub*, Sam Hamill's *Poets Against the War* anthology and *Raising Our Voices: An Anthology of Oregon Poets Against the War*. Edwards is also a regular reviewer for the literary journal, *Rain Taxi*.

In 1986, Edwards received her B.A. at Centre College in Danville, Kentucky. She secured both her M.A. and Ph.D. at the University of Louisville. Edward's professional interests include rhetoric, women's literature and poetry.